# Beyond Caring

*Trish Kerrison*

Five Leaves Publications

*for*
S · J · E · R
& *M · T*

# Contents

| | |
|---|---|
| The Ground Beneath Our Feet | 7 |
| Word on the Street (Week 1) | 8 |
| Fault Lines | 9 |
| Under the Gaze of Thomas the Tank Engine | 10 |
| No Flowers Please | 11 |
| God's Will | 12 |
| The Same Boys They Were Yesterday | 13 |
| A Baby Brother's Genetic Test | 14 |
| Brother J's Sports Day | 15 |
| Things to Do in a Wheelchair When You Are Nine | 16 |
| Putting His Shoes Away | 17 |
| An Evening In | 18 |
| Brother S Consents to Spine Surgery | 19 |
| Saint for a Day | 20 |
| Risk Assessment at the Top of Snowdon | 21 |
| Service Engineer's Visit | 22 |
| A Good Time to Retire | 23 |
| *Brother J Comments on… His Eighteenth Birthday* | 24 |
| "Is he dead yet?" | 25 |
| To the Woman on the Pier | 26 |
| Keeping Distant | 27 |
| *Brother S Comments on… Food Through a Tube* | 28 |
| The Doctor Clears His Throat | 29 |
| Blues for Brother J | 30 |
| Waiting in Intensive Care | 31 |
| Ways to Drown | 32 |
| Unravelling | 33 |
| High Dependency Unit: Inside and Out | 34 |
| *Brother S Comments on… Reaching the Age of Twenty-three* | 35 |
| The Benefits of a *Blue Peter* Childhood | 36 |
| I've Been Thinking… | 37 |
| Word on the Street (Week 1,305) | 38 |
| Co-ordination of Daily Carers | 39 |
| Beyond Caring | 40 |

**Beyond Caring**
*Trish Kerrison*

Five Leaves New Poetry #2

Published in 2023 by Five Leaves Publications
14a Long Row, Nottingham NG1 2DH
www.fiveleaves.co.uk
www.fiveleavesbookshop.co.uk

ISBN: 978-1-915434-10-4

Copyright © Trish Kerrison 2023

Cover image: "Bell Rock Lighthouse"
by J.M.W. Turner

Printed in Great Britain

It only takes
four lines
in the sand
to make a box

to put people in

to live,
contained,

until the sands shift.

**The Ground Beneath Our Feet**

The cracks were there – even as the rocks collided,
before anything was decided about dinosaurs,
or elephants or whether cats would have feathers or fur.
The cracks were there – even as gravity pulled it all together,
no-one felt the fault lines running underground,
least of all the fish emerging from the deep
and trying out their new-found feet.

The cracks were there when we apes arrived, stood upright,
learned to drive, built our roads and cities
on ground that revealed its fatal flaws too late
to save us. Hand in hand we jump
the cracks in the pavement,
laugh, even as the sands are shifting.
We walk on unsteady feet, unsteady ground.
We don't look down.

**Word on the Street (Week 1)**

    Is it catching?

                                            Perhaps they got it wrong –
                                                 get another test.

                There is nothing I can say.

You must have known
    it was in the family.

                                            Just bad luck
                                            don't think it's your fault.

                  All part of God's plan.

I know
how you feel.                          God never sends anything
                                    you can't cope with.

                Oh no…
                    Fuck.

**Fault Lines**

Somewhere in the silent past
a single gene cracks,

razor splinters scatter
down generations,

wrapped in soft beginnings,
a lethal fragment passes

mother to daughter
mother to daughter

searches,
Herod-like,
for sons.

**Under the Gaze of Thomas the Tank Engine**

From the far side of his desk,
the white coat extends a limp hand,
        then withdraws, to the safety of his notes,
announces his diagnosis,
spells out the prognosis IN NO UNCERTAIN TERMS
because it's better if he tells us everything now –

> *frequent falls – wheelchair – special school – (of course) – inability to lift – to grip – to feed oneself – curved spine – chest infections – full ventilation – bedridden – dead before eighteen.*

– so there won't be any unpleasant surprises later.

**No Flowers Please**

Cut down in youth, they deserved
a share of joy, however brief;
bride's bouquet
lover's token
finishing touch to a summer hat

not this

like flamenco dancers at a funeral,
awkward flashes of canary yellow,
sunset orange, bubble-gum pink,
blood red

they, too, must bow their heads
under grief's weight

every petal a *memento mori*,
fading, withering,

falling

**God's Will**

I can forgive, perhaps
a momentary lapse in the god
who carries all the stars upon his back,
he makes no claim on love or grief
but simply lost his grip
let the sky slip through his fingers
but how can I excuse
The One Omnipotent God
who knows what it is to lose a son?

**The Same Boys They Were Yesterday**

*Beep*
*sorry we are unable to take your call…*

we are fully occupied with building
our ginormous LEGO tower,
the biggest in the Universe, ever,
with four doors, twenty-three windows,
and every single brick we own,
because I promised…

*Beep*
*sorry, we are…*

busy with our chocolate cake,
big brother, in charge of decoration,
sorts smarties into rainbow piles,
buttercream smile smeared on face,
smaller brother puffs into icing sugar,
claps his hands in fluffy white clouds, laughs
as only a toddler can…

*Beep*
*sorry we…*

have gone to the park
to run, swing, climb, slide
before it's too late…

*Beep*
*sorry…*

**A Baby Brother's Genetic Test**

A masterclass for Cold War spies,
innocent-looking cells
stay tight-lipped in a petri dish
yielding only the trivial:
*blond hair, blue eyes, five foot six.*

Under the glare of the lamp,
DNA surrenders the codes
stashed inside the double helix.
White coats interrogate link after link,
searching for a break.

A plain brown envelope,
a single line on a pink slip:
'*No deletion or abnormality found.*'
Typed. Unsigned. No-one brave enough
to put their name to this.

**Brother J's Sports Day**

Another race, another chance to win,
he waits in his special starting place

half-way
to the finish

best foot forward
on your marks, get set…

whistle blows
muscles scream
classmates thunder past
last again

and again, and again.

*Well done for taking part!*

Loser's sticker
slapped on his shirt

ripped off
stamped on the grass over and over and over.

**Things to Do in a Wheelchair When You Are Nine**

Full speed down the pier
stop dead
close as you dare to the drop.

Little brother on the back,
mind how you go…
Quick-turn!
He's on the grass
laughing.

An art installation:
'Pile of Stones'
worth a million quid
spin the chair
back wheel skid
miss by one-hair's breadth.

Toddler brother strapped in tight
spin
faster
spin faster
spin faster faster faster
everything dizzy
world whirling
can't stop giggling
Again! Again!

Practise doughnuts on the beach
perfect your circle
repeat
on a perfectly manicured National Trust lawn.

**Putting His Shoes Away**

size three
neat
clean
in racing green
with much-loved rainbow laces
no mud
no scuffs
no footprint on the beach
no tell-tale mark on the kitchen floor
shiny oh-so-goody-two-shoes
strapped down safely on their footplates

kicking sand in my face.

**An Evening In**

I imagine you
arriving home with your dog,
cleaning her paws
so she doesn't trail mud through the hall,
tucking into your waiting meal,
toad-in-the-hole with thick gravy,
settling down to watch TV

while I, peeling potatoes
to make a shepherd's pie,
catch a whiff of something fetid,
notice a brown smear on the carpet,
bite hard on my lip
so I don't snap at the kids
and make them think it's their fault
that I must spend my tea-preparing hour
picking your dog's shit
from the tread of my son's wheelchair tyre
bit by stinking bit

with a cocktail stick.

**Brother S Consents to Spine Surgery**

Twelve years old,
he sits on the edge
legs swinging
back and forth
back and forth.

Doctors talk over his head
nuts, bolts, titanium rod
like Meccano

he nods.

But can he trust this man
who has Thursday printed on his socks
when it's Monday?

He has one question.

YES??

*Can I go sky-diving after this?*

**Saint for a Day**

7.16 am: I have patience enough
for a saint. I respond to all requests
without so much as a huff,
no matter how often a hand
needs moving up, down, left, right, forward,
back to the start, because one millimetre
makes all the difference.

I say 'just a minute' and mean it,
suppress the urge to finish his sentences,
ignore sarcastic comments.

I swear,
but only under my breath.

10.34: I am not a saint,
nor, apparently,
a very good actor.

## Risk Assessment at the Top of Snowdon

Oi!
this is a
mountain, you
can't take a wheelchair
down there, you must be insane,
two and a half thousand feet, what if
you dropped him, it shouldn't be allowed,
it's nothing short of child abuse, stop, stop, you
should be reported – OH MY GOD – you've really gone
and done it, that's so amazing, who'd have thought it, two
and a half thousand feet, an inspiration, brilliant, there should be
more people in the world like you, fantastic, let me buy you a drink

**Service Engineer's Visit**

He turns up when the computer tells him,
never used a hoist in his life. Fully qualified.

Looks about fourteen.

Came here for a stag do once,
recognises the pub.

Holds up a sling for inspection,
eager to find fault, to be first
to notice a frayed edge, a tear,
a split seam.

Thinks affairs at Derby County
have got out of hand,
more a rugby man himself.

No idea about the service needs
of four identical slings.
No, nothing on the screen.

Likes how we've done the Christmas lights.

**A Good Time to Retire**

Eighteen years in lungs;
a lifetime for some.

For him, a battle against $CO_2$,
persistent coughs, failing muscle,
as if he didn't know the war was already lost.
Unusually, he seemed to understand
'no cure' means more to live for

not less.

Secure in his knowledge,
I rested their struggling breaths
in his hands

until today.

Out of the blue,
a formal NHS letter:
'*It is a good time to retire.*'

Good for who?

*Brother J Comments on… His Eighteenth Birthday*

*One pint of cider:*
*all it takes*
*to mow down my brother*
*and run over a fence*

> **Rapid onset of drunkenness:**
> **an effect of heart medication**
> **<u>should not to be used for recreational purposes</u>**

*who knew?*

**"Is he dead yet?"**

However well met in the Ladies' queue,
a certain etiquette must be observed,
a stranger's eyes may stare at walls, or shoes,
but their ears are so much less reserved.
Between slamming doors and hand-dryer blasts
who dunnit, or didn't, might be discussed
or who's doing what with whom in the cast;
gossip washed away with the toilet flush.
But bored small-talk grows big and bold among
my not-quite-friends with their Prosecco smiles.
Caution succumbs to incontinent tongues
that let my secrets fall onto cold white tiles
like discarded tissues that lips once kissed,
as if his life was worth no more than this.

**To the Woman on the Pier**

Well done, you've caught us eating chips,
pinned me to the pier's end
while the brothers disappear
at speed,

can't believe your luck.

Gorging on your own generosity of spirit,
you regurgitate the clichés: inspiration,
God's work, reward in heaven…

You're on a roll;
your husband left you,
your daughter won't speak to you,
you hate your life, your job,
you have nothing to live for,
and now you've found someone worse off.

I respond with platitudes,
do my best to lose you.

Polite turns to ice,
you quicken your step to mine.

We are stopped,
path blocked
by the towering height
of a younger son.

*Alright, Mum?*

And you are gone.

Along with the sunset
and the chips you made me drop.

**Keeping Distant**

From a distance, I celebrate
your sons' success, happy the first
did not become the mess that was predicted.

From a distance, I'm delighted
your second son found a love
to replace the one who broke his heart.

From a distance, I'm thrilled
son number three is travelling
the world to unravel the mystery of himself.

Step closer, with lengthy letters
of Himalayan treks, of skiing trips
and I might silently think you thoughtless.

Step closer still, a tipsy late-night call
from Bondi Beach, and this time, I might let
my sadness wreck your happy-go-lucky ship.

We were once the closest friends,
from a distance,
nothing's changed.

*Brother S Comments on… Food Through a Tube*

*God, I miss fillet steak,*
*the juice, the bite of it,*

*and the crunch of apple,*
*the taste of a strawberry when you squish it,*
*the salty satisfaction of a bacon sandwich.*

*On the plus side,*
*I'm off the hook regarding spinach*
*and there's an extra little kick*
*to drinking twelve-year old Glenfiddich*
*through a straw.*

**The Doctor Clears His Throat**

Is that a cough?
Do you have an annoying bit of phlegm
at the back of your throat?
Can you shift it,
can you suck
in a litre
of air
expel it under pressure
to relieve the irritation
or is it growing, thick and fast,
a glutinous mucous plug
clogging up your airway
like a fatberg
blocking off a sewer?

Does your breath
begin to rasp,
do you turn
from choking red
to clammy grey
to blue light
that can't move fast enough?

Will they gift you a certificate:
'*cause of death: pneumonia*',
instead of '*budget manager who,
when drawing his line in the sand,
found, in this unremarkable case,
that a four-thousand-pound cough-assistor
was a luxury too far?*'

**Blues for Brother J**

Midnight blue:
notes fade
on Billy Bragg's guitar

Grey-blue:
lips of a young man
who can no longer catch
a breath

Steely-blue:
words of panic     of terror

Cornflower blue:
eyes fixed on mine

Electric blue:
light scythes through dark,
sirens blaring

Ice blue:
screen flashes
oxygen level     falling

Sapphire blue:
glimpse of dawn
through tinted windows
as we jump red lights

**Waiting in Intensive Care**

Not much of a knitter, me.
*Knit one. Purl one.*
Not like Nanna – needles always clicking,
even Hitler couldn't stop her.

Bootees, hats, jumpers.
*Knit one. Purl one.*
Three pairs of socks every week
for the feet of a homesick soldier.

I wish I'd learned the stitches,
*Knit one. Purl one. Slip one.*
understood the click, click, click
of her bloody-minded spirit.

She would not sit here, useless,
*Knit one. Purl one. Slip one. Knit one.*
forgetting to breathe, staring at the monitor,
bargaining with God, or whoever.

*Knit one.*
And another and another and another and keep going
until he wakes up and laughs at this stringy red scarfy-thing
he wouldn't be seen dead in.

*Knit one. Slip one. Drop one. Drop one. Drop*
Unravel.

**Ways to Drown**

It's easy:
allow shifting sands to take hold,
to get a grip on ankles, knees, shins,
to slowly squeeze the life out of you,
until, in terror of your soul going under,
you kick and thrash about in a frenzy
that drags you further down

It's easy to drown:
stand still,
wait
for a wish to be granted,
a prayer to be answered,
a lifeboat to appear on the horizon

It's easy to drown:
if you don't know how to save yourself

if no-one ever taught you to lie flush
with the sand, to  spread  your  weight,
low and flat, like a s t a r f i s h,
to     slip     sideways     across     the         surface
with     exquisite     slowness
inch     by     precarious     inch
back     to     land

It's easy to drown:
when you no longer know where land is.

**Unravelling**

A family of six
cannot learn to be five

if I hold on tight,
you can't leave –

our joker in the pack
out-of-the-box thinker
(advice on all things tech)

festival goer
(mind your toes in the mosh-pit)
team-player, footballer, coach
nerve-of-steel penalty-taker

delirious at Wembley
you despair at Derby County
try it on at Scrabble
clean-up at Monopoly

our wildlife expert
owl enthusiast
any dog's best friend

try anything once:
dangle from a zip-wire
head first on a slide
daredevil on a trike

our sailor in a laundry basket
sand boat, rock pool
splash and grab

bedtime hugs
*Going on a Bear Hunt*

our beautiful white-blond baby,
fingers curled round mine

hold on

**High Dependency Unit: Inside and Out**

Tea trolley rattles
night into day
the ventilator breathes

>*in the calm of the morning*
>*high viz and hard hat swarm*

risk-assess, plan

every breath
restores him
with a gentle shush

>*the crew are called*
>*make final preparations*

no room for error

measure, check, report
adjust the dials
deep breath

>*cranes synchronise*
>*and lift, dead weight*

hangs in the air

he breathes
with the machine
in perfect harmony

>*green light signals*
>*proceed*
>*the cornerstone inches home*

every move monitored

on the screen, his breaths
a neat line of zig-zag stitching

>holding all the pieces in place.

### *Brother S Comments on… Reaching the Age of Twenty-Three*

*Twenty-three candles I can't blow out*
*for a birthday they said I wouldn't see*

*something to celebrate*

*like a pair of deflated balloons*
*my lungs won't rise to the occasion*

*I can raise a smile, or an eyebrow*
*can't raise my glass*

*my skeleton still hangs together, no matter*
*that tendons can no longer be trusted*

*the ball has fallen out with the socket*
*my carpals have all curled up*

*in one last-ditched attempt*
*to get a grip*

*with no-one pulling the strings*

*bones choose to stay loosely connected*
*if a little experimental*

*my femur leans outwards*
*at an unprecedented angle*

*one knee turns in on itself*
*while the other looks away*

*my feet flop – sideways, downwards,*
*like a puppet*

*dropped back in its box.*

**The Benefits of a *Blue Peter* Childhood**

It was the matchbox and the yoghurt pot,
sticky-back plasticked into dolls' house furniture,
that led to the realisation, half a century later, that a bag,
designed for the long-term storage of blankets,
was made from exactly the sort of semi-rigid plastic
that could be reconfigured as a tunnel structure,
and, with the aid of Velcro and gaffer tape, fashioned
into a wind-and-hail-and-rain-proof hand cover
so a young man might drive his wheelchair
to outdoor festivals and parties in the park
unimpeded by the vagaries of British weather,
and all for the sum of two pound thirty-seven
instead of three hundred dollars for the off-the-peg
version imported from America.

**I've Been Thinking…**

about that picture: you standing,
grinning, with your brother,
either side of Mickey Mouse, no sign
of a wheelchair

and about your childhood: how we had
a government that believed in your worth,
put our money where its mouth was:
school support, access ramp, dropped kerb,
and although it wasn't perfect,
it felt like progress

and about the austerity years, how freely
they spoke empty words of equality and diversity
while pulling tight on the purse strings

and about how easily things slip,
how help becomes unfair advantage,
access a threat to business, a ramp
a trip hazard for the able-bodied,
and how what we thought was progress

was a blip

and how COVID blew equality out of the water
and ministers on daytime TV thought it OK
to say there would be no ICU beds
for people like you

and about how you fought your way back
to life, how you dyed
your hair purple,
got a tattoo,
went to live gigs
without waiting for Government approval

and how,
in the picture you just pinged to my phone,
you're grinning.

**Word on the Street (Week 1,305)**

Can I just say,
it's amazing what you do.

What a lovely day to bring them out.

How come there's a pair of them,
are they alright, you know, 'upstairs'?

Aren't they cute!

*Here, let me lift that for you…no?*
*                              ungrateful bitch.*

Three boys and a girl,
you'll be left with one of each in the end then.
That's nice.

I've done disability –
my mother had arthritis.

You're such an angel,
God's lesson to us all.

*You can't unload a wheelchair here,*
*get that fucking vehicle out of my road.*

Can I just say,
you're an inspiration, you are.

## Co-ordination of Daily Carers

Am I a spider,
that I so deftly draw together strands
of other lives to make my web?
How expertly I tease out clues
from their coffee-break chat, weave
their plans into the pattern of my safety net.
I am vigilant, hourly I inspect
each delicate thread, my life on hold,
to darn and mend the breaks and tears
that would see it all unravel.

Or am I a bluebottle, caught in a web
of my own carelessness? Distracted
by sun shimmering on my iridescent blue,
did I forget, for once, to look ahead?
Wings tight-bound, do I admit defeat,
or can I still dream of flight?

Or am I a housefly, just bright enough
to know when I am beaten,
but without the wisdom
to cease the fight?

**Beyond Caring**

*after Eiléan Ni Chuilleanáin*

When we go our separate ways,
I will take up a life by the sea,
dawdle through day after endless day,
watching how tides ebb and flow
without reference.

I will have a phone that isn't smart,

I will kick along the water's edge
on a beach devoid of warnings, red flags,
byelaws. I will search the sand for cockles
with their shells clamped shut, observe crabs
as they scuttle from one rockpool to another,
find comfort in the familiar screech of gulls.

I will watch sail-boats scudding across the surf,
feel silk ribbons of seaweed under my feet,
run my fingers over barnacle-roughened rocks,
fill my lungs with gulps of salty air, scream
into the wind until the sound is lost.

I will swim then,
easy loose-limbed strokes all the way
to the lighthouse, looking back only
to marvel at how far I have come.